The OPENAI API Contract Analyst's Codebook

Methods for Designing an AI-Powered Solution

Author: Mark J Davenport

While every precaution has been taken in the preparation of this book, the publisher assumes no responsibility for errors or omissions, or for damages resulting from the use of the information contained herein.

AI UNLOCKED: BUILDING AN OPENAI-API DOCUMENT ANALYSIS ENGINE

First edition. September 22, 2024.

ISBN: 979-8227647566

Written by Mark Davenport.

Introduction to Leveraging OpenAI API for Large Document Processing

In this section, we explore how I employed the OpenAI API to efficiently analyze and process legal documents of varying lengths, from a few pages to well over a hundred pages. The focus will be on overcoming token limitations while maintaining accuracy and context in document analysis. I will explain the various methods used, including chain-of-thought reasoning and the application of segmentation techniques to break down large documents into manageable sections. The solution also incorporates techniques for summarization and key data extraction to ensure comprehensive coverage of the content, even when dealing with large-scale input.

We will cover the following areas in detail:

1. **Understanding Token Limits in the OpenAI API**: How to recognize and manage token constraints inherent to the API and effectively process documents exceeding those limits.

2. **Document Segmentation**: The step-by-step method I used to break large documents into smaller chunks to ensure all critical data is processed without overloading the API.

3. **Chain-of-Thought Processing**: Utilizing incremental prompts and chained results to maintain document coherence across multiple API calls.

4. **Summarization and Key Data Extraction**: How I used summarization techniques to distill long, complex legal documents into their essential components while preserving important details.

5. **Optimizing Performance**: Code and techniques developed to enhance API performance when dealing with documents, ensuring quick and accurate responses without token overflows.

6. **Practical Examples and Application**: Real-world applications

of the techniques described, focusing on how they are used for contract analysis and the benefits they provide for legal professionals and businesses alike.

By the end of this section, you will have a detailed understanding of how to work with the OpenAI API in environments where token limits present challenges, and you will be able to implement similar strategies in your own projects for handling large-scale document analysis.

Understanding Token Limits in the OpenAI API

The first and most significant challenge when working with the OpenAI API for large document processing is managing the token limits imposed by the system. The OpenAI API uses a token-based system where each word, punctuation, and even certain characters are counted as tokens. The API has limits on the number of tokens that can be processed at once, depending on the model used. For instance, GPT-3 has a token limit of 4096 tokens, while GPT-4 can handle up to 8,000 tokens or more, depending on the specific version.

When working with documents that exceed these limits, it's critical to adopt strategies that allow processing to be done in segments without losing the context and flow of the document.

Key Token Management Techniques

1. **Document Length Assessment**: Before submitting a document to the API, it's essential to assess its length in terms of tokens. This can be done using a token counter that simulates how the API counts tokens. Knowing the token count helps to strategize how the document can be divided and processed.

2. **Chunking the Document**: For documents exceeding the token limit, I employed a method known as "chunking." This involved breaking the document into smaller, manageable sections, each within the allowed token limit. The key here is to ensure that each chunk contains a logically complete section of

the document, such as a full clause or a well-rounded paragraph, so that the context remains intact.

3. **Maintaining Context Across Chunks**: One of the primary challenges with chunking is maintaining context when transitioning between chunks. To overcome this, I designed the system to overlap a small portion of each chunk with the preceding and following sections. This way, the API retains a sense of continuity between related sections, which is especially important for documents like contracts where terms may reference one another.

4. **Using Headers and Meta Information**: Another technique I used was to prepend each chunk with headers or meta information that provided essential context for the API. For example, if processing a section of a contract, the heading for that section (e.g., "Payment Terms") would be sent along with the chunk, allowing the API to "understand" the context of the following text.

Example of Token Chunking in Practice

Here's a simplified example of how a legal document might be divided into chunks for processing by the API:

text
Copy code
Chunk 1:
Header: "Payment Terms"
Text: "The payment for services shall be made within thirty (30) days of receiving an invoice, provided that all..."
(contains 300 tokens)
Chunk 2:
Header: "Payment Terms - continued"
Text: "terms and conditions are satisfied. In the event of any dispute regarding the invoice, the client shall notify..."

(overlap of 20 tokens from the previous chunk for continuity, total 350 tokens)

Chunk 3:

Header: "Liability Limitation"

Text: "Neither party shall be liable for indirect, incidental, or consequential damages arising from this agreement..."

(350 tokens)

By using this chunking method, I was able to process large documents while ensuring that the context between different sections was preserved. Additionally, each chunk was tagged with relevant headings so that the API could better understand the legal or contractual significance of each part of the document.

Token-Saving Techniques

When working with large documents, it's also essential to adopt token-saving techniques to maximize the use of the available limit. Some of these techniques include:

- **Avoiding Redundant Information**: When summarizing or processing a document, I programmed the system to avoid re-processing parts of the document that had already been summarized or analyzed, saving token usage for new and relevant information.

- **Summarization Before Processing**: In some cases, I used summarization techniques to condense particularly verbose sections of the document. This was especially useful when dealing with boilerplate text in contracts that didn't require in-depth analysis but still needed to be referenced.

- **Selective Analysis**: Not every part of a document always needs the same level of analysis. I developed a method to selectively choose which sections to analyze deeply and which to process lightly based on key phrases or headings, further optimizing token usage.

In the next section, we'll explore how I employed **Document Segmentation** to break down and categorize large documents into logical parts for efficient processing.

Document Segmentation for Large-Scale Processing

After recognizing the token limitations, the next critical step in efficiently processing large documents using the OpenAI API is **Document Segmentation**. This method involves breaking down the document into logical and manageable sections, which not only makes it easier to process within the token limits but also ensures that the context of each part of the document is preserved and processed meaningfully.

Document segmentation goes beyond simple chunking, as it requires a more nuanced approach to understanding the structure and organization of the document. For legal and contractual documents, segmentation must take into account the significance of clauses, sections, and headings, ensuring that critical information is kept together during the API's processing.

Key Strategies for Effective Document Segmentation

1. **Understanding Document Structure**: Legal documents, such as contracts, tend to follow a specific structure with headings, clauses, and subsections. I utilized this natural structure to inform the segmentation process, ensuring that related sections were kept together. For example, a section on "Liability" would be processed as one chunk, even if it required breaking it into smaller segments.

2. **Hierarchical Segmentation**: Documents were first broken down at a high level, based on major sections such as:
   - **Introduction or Recitals**
   - **Definitions**
   - **Terms and Conditions**
   - **Liability Clauses**
   - **Termination Clauses**

    ◦ **Miscellaneous Provisions**

Within each major section, further subdivision was applied to keep the text under the token limit. For example, within the "Terms and Conditions" section, individual clauses like payment terms, delivery obligations, and service level agreements were each treated as separate chunks.

1. **Using Section Markers**: I employed clear section markers or headings for each chunk to maintain the logical flow and context. When breaking down a document, I added these markers to ensure that each chunk's content was properly understood by the API, retaining the same meaning as if it were processed in a single request. For instance, each segmented chunk was introduced with its section title, followed by the relevant text.

2. **Segmenting by Legal Clauses and Logical Breaks**: When processing contracts, each legal clause was treated as a distinct logical unit. This ensured that the legal meaning was preserved in its entirety within a single chunk, avoiding potential misinterpretation if the clause were split between chunks. I paid close attention to punctuation and sentence breaks to maintain clarity.

Example: Segmenting a Contract for Processing
Consider a contract with the following sections:

- **1. Introduction**
- **2. Definitions**
- **3. Payment Terms**
- **4. Confidentiality**
- **5. Liability Limitations**
- **6. Termination Clauses**

This structure allowed me to segment the document into logical chunks based on its natural breakdown. For instance:

Chunk 1: (Introduction)

"Whereas the parties... agree to the terms and conditions outlined below, commencing on the 1st of January..."

Chunk 2: (Definitions)

"Definitions: 'Client' refers to... 'Service Provider' means... (continues with definitions)..."

Chunk 3: (Payment Terms)

"Payment Terms: The payment shall be made within thirty (30) days of invoice receipt... (350 tokens)"

Chunk 4: (Payment Terms - Continued)

"In the event of any dispute, the client shall notify... (overlap of 20 tokens for context continuity)"

Chunk 5: (Confidentiality)

"The parties agree to maintain confidentiality of all information disclosed... (350 tokens)"

Chunk 6: (Liability Limitations)

"Neither party shall be liable for incidental damages arising out of this agreement... (350 tokens)"

In this example, I used logical breaks between sections and sub-sections to preserve meaning. Sections like "Payment Terms" or "Liability Limitations" often contain critical clauses that require careful segmentation. By doing so, I ensured that the API could analyze the text while keeping its integrity intact.

Benefits of Document Segmentation

1. **Context Preservation**: Segmenting by logical sections allowed the API to process text without losing the overall context. By sending coherent chunks, each segment could be understood in full, allowing the API to generate more accurate outputs, such as summaries, analysis, or responses.

2. **Reduced Overload**: Segmenting large documents into smaller sections helped avoid overwhelming the API and prevented token overflow. By keeping each chunk within the token limit,

I ensured that the entire document could be processed efficiently without errors or dropped content.

3. **Enhanced Focus on Key Areas**: Some parts of a document may require more detailed analysis than others. Segmenting allowed for prioritizing critical sections (e.g., liability clauses) for deeper analysis, while less important sections could be processed more lightly or summarized. This approach optimized the API's performance and saved tokens.

4. **Maintaining Legal Integrity**: Legal documents have a specific flow and interconnectedness between clauses. Proper segmentation ensures that clauses referring to one another (e.g., termination referring to liability) remain meaningful and connected, even when processed separately. I also incorporated overlaps between related sections to ensure the document's legal coherence remained intact.

Technical Implementation of Segmentation

The segmentation process required a combination of manual logic and automated tools. Here's how I approached it:

- **Automatic Detection of Headings and Sections**: For many contracts and legal documents, headings are formatted in distinct ways (bold, numbered, or capitalized). I wrote a script that automatically detected these headings and used them to segment the document accordingly.

- **Chunk Size Calculation**: To ensure that each chunk fit within the token limit, I wrote a utility to calculate the number of tokens in a given segment. If a section exceeded the token limit, the utility would suggest breakpoints based on sentence endings or punctuation, minimizing disruption to the text flow.

- **Overlapping Chunks for Continuity**: When breaking a

section into multiple chunks, the last few sentences of the previous chunk were carried over into the next. This overlap helped maintain continuity for the API, ensuring it didn't lose context when processing related clauses.

Example of Overlap for Continuity

Here's how overlapping was applied between two chunks:

Chunk 3: (Payment Terms)

"The payment shall be made within thirty (30) days of invoice receipt..."

Chunk 4: (Payment Terms - Continued)

"In the event of any dispute regarding the invoice, the client shall notify the provider in writing..."

Overlap: The last few sentences from Chunk 3 are repeated in Chunk 4 to maintain the flow, ensuring no context is lost.

This segmentation approach allowed for processing even the largest legal documents within the token constraints while retaining the integrity and meaning of the document. In the next section, we will explore how I employed **Chain-of-Thought Processing** to link segments together, ensuring continuity and coherence in multi-step analyses.

Chain-of-Thought Processing: A Method to Maintain Continuity

Chain-of-thought processing is a technique used to handle complex tasks and large amounts of information in a step-by-step manner, ensuring that each part of the input is processed logically and that the system maintains coherence across multiple steps or chunks of data.

When applied to working with the OpenAI API for large documents, chain-of-thought processing helps maintain context and coherence across multiple API calls, especially when the text exceeds token limits. Essentially, this method involves breaking down a large task into smaller, manageable steps (or chunks) and ensuring that each step builds upon the previous one. This approach is especially useful when working with lengthy and interconnected documents, such as legal contracts.

How Chain-of-Thought Works

The idea behind chain-of-thought processing is similar to how humans approach complex tasks: one step at a time, but always keeping in mind what has been done previously to inform the next step. Here's how it works in practice:

1. **Step-by-Step Processing**: The document is broken down into smaller segments, and each segment is processed separately by the API. The results of each step are then used to inform the next API call.

2. **Preserving Context Across Chunks**: To ensure that the API understands the broader context, important information from previous chunks is carried over to the next API call. This might include summaries, key terms, or important points that were extracted from earlier segments. In this way, each chunk benefits from the knowledge and context of previous ones, resulting in a more coherent overall output.

3. **Incremental Summarization and Analysis**: At each step of processing, summarization or analysis can be done on the current chunk. These results are then appended to or integrated with the summaries from previous chunks. By the end, a full document summary or analysis is created from all the smaller parts, maintaining the logical flow of the original document.

4. **Handling Dependencies**: In documents like contracts, some sections depend heavily on others. For example, a section on "Termination" may reference clauses from "Liability" or "Payment Terms." Chain-of-thought processing ensures that these dependencies are preserved, as each chunk is processed in sequence, with key details passed forward as necessary.

Key Components of Chain-of-Thought Processing

1. **Logical Flow**: Every chunk of the document is processed in the order it appears, with context built up over time. The logical flow ensures that the API can understand how different sections of the document are related.

2. **Recursive Summarization**: Each processed chunk can be summarized, and the resulting summary becomes part of the context for the next chunk. For example, after processing "Payment Terms," the API might generate a brief summary of the terms, which is then used when processing the next section, "Liability."

3. **Overlapping Context**: Just as in segmentation, chain-of-thought processing often requires an overlap between chunks. This overlap ensures that the API is not working in isolation on any particular chunk but instead has access to key information from the previous section.

Practical Example of Chain-of-Thought in Legal Documents

Consider the scenario of analyzing a legal contract with multiple interconnected sections. Here's how chain-of-thought processing might work:

- **Chunk 1: Payment Terms**
  - The API processes the payment terms and generates a summary: "Payments are due within 30 days, with a 10% late fee applied after that."
- **Chunk 2: Liability Limitations**
  - The summary of the payment terms is passed as part of the context for the liability section. This allows the API to recognize any potential conflicts or dependencies between these sections: "Liability is limited to 10% of unpaid invoices."

- **Chunk 3: Termination Clauses**
  - ○ When processing the termination clauses, the API is aware of the payment and liability terms already analyzed. If the termination section refers to these clauses, the system can understand their relevance: "Termination can occur if payments are 60 days overdue or if liabilities exceed contractual limits."

At each step, chain-of-thought processing ensures that the API "remembers" the context of the document, even when processing separate chunks. This leads to more accurate summaries, analyses, and understanding of the document as a whole.

Advantages of Chain-of-Thought Processing

1. **Maintaining Continuity in Large Documents**: Chain-of-thought processing is essential when token limits force us to split large documents into smaller sections. This method ensures that each section is understood in the context of the entire document, rather than in isolation.
2. **Enhanced Accuracy**: By building up context incrementally, the API can provide more accurate responses, summaries, and analyses. Each step benefits from the previous one, reducing the risk of errors due to missing context.
3. **Improved Legal and Contractual Analysis**: Legal documents often contain interdependencies between sections, such as references to terms, conditions, and clauses located elsewhere in the document. Chain-of-thought processing ensures that these connections are preserved, resulting in a more thorough analysis of the document.

Technical Implementation of Chain-of-Thought Processing

To implement chain-of-thought processing, I developed a system where:

ᴜtate Information is Carried Over: After each API call, critical information such as extracted summaries, key terms, and important clauses is saved. This data is then appended to the next chunk, ensuring that the API understands how the sections are related.

- **Recursive API Calls**: The document is processed recursively, with each API call building on the output of the previous one. This recursive process continues until the entire document is processed.

- **Summarization of Each Section**: After processing each section, the API generates a brief summary or key insights, which are saved and passed forward to the next section for enhanced understanding.

Chain-of-thought processing is an essential technique for handling large-scale documents when token limitations prevent single-shot processing. By breaking down the task into smaller steps and carrying context forward, the API can process documents with greater accuracy and coherence.

Next, we'll discuss **Summarization and Key Data Extraction**, a crucial part of ensuring that important information is distilled from large documents, making them more manageable and easier to analyze.

Summarization and Key Data Extraction: Streamlining Large Document Processing

Summarization is the process of condensing a large amount of information into a shorter, more manageable form while retaining the essential meaning and critical details. When working with large documents, summarization helps reduce the amount of text that needs to be processed by the OpenAI API, allowing key insights and information to be extracted efficiently within token limits.

In the context of using the OpenAI API, summarization is invaluable for handling large legal or technical documents. By extracting the core content from each section of a document and summarizing it, the system can provide a high-level understanding while preserving important details, such as key terms, obligations, and conditions.

How Summarization Works in Document Processing

Summarization is typically performed in two stages:

1. **Segment-Level Summarization**: As each chunk or section of the document is processed, the API generates a brief summary of that chunk. This summary includes the main points or arguments presented in the section, ensuring that nothing essential is lost.

2. **Global Summarization**: After all segments of the document have been processed, the individual summaries are combined to create a global summary of the entire document. This summary captures the full scope of the document while being much more concise than the original.

This two-step process ensures that the document is comprehensively summarized while adhering to token constraints.

Different Types of Summarization

1. **Extractive Summarization**: In extractive summarization, the most important sentences or phrases from the document are selected and presented as the summary. This approach is useful when specific wording or phrasing is important, such as in legal documents where precise language matters. The challenge with extractive summarization is that it may not always flow smoothly since the sentences are directly taken from the original text.

2. **Abstractive Summarization**: Abstractive summarization, which is commonly used in modern AI, involves generating new sentences that convey the same meaning as the original text. This method allows for more natural and fluid summaries.

and readable
oth

n the exact
ractive
l sections.

n OpenAI API

step in summarizing a section
g its key points. I designed prompts
cus on extracting the most critical
obligations, dates, clauses, and
epending on the document's type. For
contract, payment terms, termination clauses, and
mitations are often key sections that need precise
aries.

ompt Design for Focused Summarization: Crafting effective prompts was crucial to ensure that the API generated useful summaries. I included instructions in the prompts to prioritize specific types of information based on the document's context. For example, if the document was a legal contract, the prompt would instruct the API to summarize key terms, legal obligations, and any risk factors mentioned.

Example prompt for summarizing a section:
text
Copy code
Summarize the following text. Focus on identifying any legal obligations, payment terms, liability clauses, and deadlines:

"The payment for services shall be r
receiving the invoice. If the payment is del

1. **Context-Aware Summarization**: T
   of maintaining context within a singl
   large documents processed in chunks,
   the necessary context in each API call by
   key points from previous sections. This en
   could understand the broader context and
   coherent summaries.

2. **Summarizing Sections with Overlapping In**
   many legal or technical documents, sections ca
   reference each other. When summarizing these se
   implemented a method where previously summari
   were included as context in the prompt for the next
   This helped maintain continuity and prevented the lo
   interconnected information.

Example of Summarization in Practice

Let's look at a simplified example of how summarization works
a legal contract:

Original Text (Payment Terms):

text

Copy code

The payment for services shall be made within thirty (30) days of receiving an invoice from the provider. If the client fails to make payment within this period, a late fee of 5% will be applied to the outstanding balance. Should the payment remain overdue for more than 60 days, the provider reserves the right to terminate the agreement immediately, without any further obligation to the client.

Extractive Summary:

text

Copy code

- Payment must be made within 30 days of invoice.
- A 5% late fee applies if payment is delayed.
- Agreement may be terminated if payment is overdue by more than 60 days.

Abstractive Summary:

text

Copy code

Clients are required to pay invoices within 30 days. Failure to do so results in a 5% penalty, and if payments are more than 60 days late, the provider can terminate the contract.

In both the extractive and abstractive examples, the key points of the payment terms are retained, but the abstractive summary is more natural and fluid, whereas the extractive summary preserves the original phrasing.

Summarization of Complex Clauses

For more complex sections, such as liability or indemnity clauses, I focused on preserving the legal meaning without overwhelming detail. For example:

Original Text (Liability Limitation):

text

Copy code

Neither party shall be liable to the other for any indirect, incidental, special, or consequential damages, including but not limited to lost profits, arising out of or in connection with this agreement, even if such party has been advised of the possibility of such damages. The total liability of each party under this agreement shall not exceed the total fees paid by the client during the preceding 12 months.

Summary:

text

Copy code

- Neither party is liable for indirect damages (e.g., lost profits).
- Total liability is capped at the fees paid in the last 12 months.

Here, the summarization focuses on the essential points of the liability clause, helping users quickly understand the limits of legal responsibility without having to process the detailed legal language.

Benefits of Summarization in Large Document Processing

1. **Token Efficiency**: Summarization drastically reduces the number of tokens that need to be processed by the API. By condensing long sections of text, I was able to save tokens, allowing for more comprehensive analysis of larger documents within the token limits.

2. **Enhanced Readability**: Summarized sections are easier to read and understand, especially for those who may not be familiar with legal or technical jargon. This makes summarization particularly useful when sharing key insights with stakeholders who need a high-level understanding without getting lost in the details.

3. **Faster Processing**: By summarizing sections before they are analyzed in depth, I optimized the speed and efficiency of the document processing pipeline. Summaries provided a quick way to assess the most important parts of the document, reducing the time spent on less critical sections.

4. **Scalability**: Summarization made it possible to scale document processing across multiple large documents, such as contracts or lengthy reports. Rather than being constrained by the token limits of individual API calls, I could summarize and process documents in stages, combining the results into a cohesive whole.

Summarization as Part of the Full Processing Workflow

Summarization was integrated into the broader workflow of document processing. As I processed each chunk of a document, I generated summaries that were stored and used for later stages, such as:

- **Summarization before Analysis**: Before diving deep into the legal analysis, I generated a summary of each section to get an overview. This helped guide which parts of the document required more detailed attention.
- **Summarization for Output**: After processing the entire document, I combined the section summaries into a final output, providing an executive summary of the whole document. This was especially useful for users who needed a concise version of the document's key points.

Summarization is a powerful tool that streamlines the processing of large documents by condensing essential information, improving efficiency, and ensuring that key details are preserved. It plays a vital role in managing token limits while maintaining the accuracy and comprehensiveness of the analysis.

In the next section, we will explore **Optimizing Performance**, where I discuss the techniques used to ensure efficient processing and performance when dealing with large-scale documents and complex queries.

Optimizing Performance for Large Document Processing

When processing large documents with the OpenAI API, optimization is essential to ensure that the system runs efficiently, avoids token overflows, and delivers quick, accurate results. Large-scale documents, such as contracts or legal briefs, can be resource-intensive to process, so applying the right techniques to optimize performance becomes crucial. In this section, I will explain the methods I used to optimize the performance of document analysis while maintaining accuracy and coherence across multiple API calls.

Key Optimization Strategies

1. **Selective Processing of Sections**: Not all parts of a document require the same level of processing. Some sections may be

standard legal boilerplate (e.g., "Governing Law" or "Severability"), while others, like "Payment Terms" or "Liability Clauses," may need more detailed analysis. To optimize performance, I categorized sections by their importance or complexity and applied more detailed processing to critical sections while using lighter processing or summarization for less important sections.

For example:

- **Full Analysis** for critical sections like "Termination Clauses" or "Liability Limitations."
- **Light Summarization** for less complex or boilerplate sections like "Governing Law."

This selective approach allowed me to allocate more tokens and processing power where it mattered most, avoiding unnecessary resource consumption on unimportant parts of the document.

1. **Efficient Token Usage**: Managing tokens efficiently is crucial to optimizing performance. Here are the techniques I used to reduce token consumption:
   - **Pre-Summarization**: Before diving deep into long sections, I ran initial summarization steps to reduce their length. By summarizing verbose sections early on, I decreased the number of tokens that needed to be processed in later stages.
   - **Removing Redundant Data**: Legal documents often contain redundant information, such as repeated clauses or definitions. I implemented a check to identify and avoid processing the same content multiple times. This prevented wasting tokens on

duplicated sections.

- ◦ **Data Compression**: When sending context or summaries to the API, I focused on compressing the information to only the most essential details. For example, instead of passing the full text of a previously processed section, I sent a concise summary that provided enough context without overloading the token limit.

2. **Parallel Processing**: For large documents, I employed parallel processing where multiple sections could be processed simultaneously, particularly when those sections were independent of one another. This approach dramatically sped up the overall analysis by distributing the workload across multiple API calls.

   - ◦ **Non-Dependent Sections**: Sections that didn't rely on each other for context were processed in parallel. For example, the "Payment Terms" and "Confidentiality" sections of a contract can be processed independently since they rarely affect each other's meaning.

   - ◦ **Batching Small Sections**: Smaller sections of a document, such as short clauses or definitions, were grouped together and processed as a batch. This optimized API calls by using the token limit efficiently without needing to handle each small section separately.

3. **Caching and Reusing Results**: I implemented a caching mechanism to store and reuse results from sections that had already been processed. This was particularly useful for:

   - ◦ **Common Phrases or Clauses**: Contracts often include standard legal language. If a clause had already been processed in a previous document, I retrieved the cached analysis or summary instead of reprocessing the same content.

- **Context Carry-Over**: When working through large documents, the context from previous API calls (e.g., summaries or key points) was cached and reused to provide continuity in subsequent sections, reducing redundant API usage.

4. **Dynamic Chunking**: Chunking the document into parts that fit within the token limit is a common method, but dynamic chunking goes further by adjusting the chunk size based on the complexity of the text. For simpler sections, larger chunks were processed at once, maximizing the token usage. For more complex sections that required detailed analysis, smaller chunks were used to avoid overwhelming the API and to ensure more focused processing.

   - **Simple Sections**: For sections like "Definitions" or straightforward terms, I could bundle more content into a single chunk.
   - **Complex Clauses**: For sections with legal nuance, I reduced the chunk size and applied more detailed analysis, ensuring accuracy without overloading the API.

5. **Layered Summarization**: Layered summarization is a technique where the document is summarized multiple times at different stages of processing. This ensures that as each layer of the document is processed, the summarization becomes more refined, allowing for better control over token usage while still capturing the core details.

   - **First Pass Summary**: Initially, large sections of the document are summarized at a high level to capture the general meaning.

- **Second Pass Summary**: For critical sections, a more detailed summary is generated, providing additional context or clarifications where needed.
- **Final Layer**: After all sections have been processed, a final global summary is created, incorporating the details from the previous passes but in a highly condensed form.

6. **Using the API's Output Efficiently**: In some cases, the API's response might be more verbose than necessary. I used post-processing techniques to further condense the output:
   - **Post-Processing Pruning**: After receiving the API's response, I removed any redundant or unnecessary information, keeping only the most critical parts of the response.
   - **Streamlining Summaries**: Even after summarization, there can be irrelevant details or filler language. By refining the API's output manually or programmatically, I produced more concise and to-the-point summaries.

7. **Error Handling and Recovery**: Handling large documents can sometimes cause the API to return incomplete results or errors due to token overloads or unexpected input. I implemented error handling and recovery strategies to ensure smooth operation:
   - **Auto-Chunking on Failure**: If a section caused an error due to excessive length, the system automatically re-chunked that section into smaller parts and retried the API call.
   - **Token Overflow Prevention**: I included a check to ensure that no single API call exceeded the token limit. If the system detected that a chunk was too

large, it would be dynamically resized to prevent errors.

- ◦ **Fallback Logic**: In case of repeated failures, I implemented fallback logic that simplified the text or generated more abstract summaries as a temporary solution until a more detailed analysis could be performed.

Example of Optimization in Action

Let's consider a large legal contract with multiple complex sections:

Original Approach (Without Optimization):

- Each section is processed individually, regardless of size or importance.
- No caching or parallel processing is used, meaning redundant sections are reprocessed each time.
- Each API call includes the full context of the document, leading to token overflows or inefficiencies.

Optimized Approach:

- Sections like "Governing Law" or "Severability" are grouped and processed in a single API call since they require minimal analysis.
- Critical sections, like "Liability" and "Payment Terms," are processed with more granularity, but dynamic chunking is applied to keep token usage efficient.
- Summaries from previous sections are cached and reused to prevent redundancy.
- Parallel processing allows multiple independent sections to be analyzed simultaneously, reducing overall processing time by 30–40%.

Performance Gains from Optimization

By applying these optimizations, I was able to achieve several key performance improvements:

- **Reduced Processing Time**: Parallel processing and selective analysis reduced the time required to analyze a large document by 30–50%, depending on its complexity.
- **Minimized Token Usage**: Efficient token management, including pre-summarization and dynamic chunking, resulted in fewer API calls, reducing overall token consumption by 20–40%.
- **Improved Accuracy**: By focusing the API's processing power on critical sections, the final output was more accurate and detailed where it mattered most, while less important sections were still covered adequately.
- **Error Reduction**: Proactive error handling and chunk resizing minimized the number of failed API calls, improving the overall reliability of the system.

Optimizing performance is essential when dealing with large-scale document analysis using the OpenAI API. By employing techniques like selective processing, dynamic chunking, parallel processing, and caching, I was able to ensure that even the largest and most complex documents were processed efficiently without compromising on accuracy or detail.

Next, we will move on to **Practical Examples and Application**, where I will showcase how these techniques were applied in real-world scenarios, particularly in contract analysis and document review.

Practical Examples and Application: Leveraging Optimized OpenAI API Processing

In this section, I will demonstrate the practical application of the techniques discussed so far, showing how these strategies can be used in real-world scenarios, particularly for legal document analysis and contract review. These examples illustrate how I successfully processed large and complex documents using the OpenAI API, managing token limits, and ensuring accurate and meaningful analysis.

Example 1: Analyzing a Multi-Section Legal Contract

One of the most common tasks in document processing involves analyzing a contract that spans dozens or even hundreds of pages, with numerous clauses and sections. Each section may include critical legal obligations, and some sections reference others, making it essential to maintain context throughout the document.

Scenario: A legal firm needs to review a 50-page service agreement that includes sections on payment terms, liability limitations, confidentiality, and termination clauses. The goal is to summarize key points and highlight any areas that may pose a legal risk to their client.

Steps Taken:

1. **Document Segmentation**: The document is divided into logical sections based on its structure, such as:
   - **Introduction**
   - **Payment Terms**
   - **Confidentiality Clause**
   - **Liability Limitations**
   - **Termination Clause**

Each section is then processed individually using the OpenAI API.

1. **Selective Processing:**
   - The **Introduction** and **Governing Law** sections are processed using a summarization-only approach, as they contain standard legal boilerplate.
   - The **Payment Terms** and **Liability Limitations** sections are flagged for deeper analysis since they

contain specific financial and legal risks that need to be assessed.

2. **Chain-of-Thought for Legal Coherence**:
   - Each section is processed in sequence, with key points from the previous sections carried forward as context to ensure the API understands interdependencies. For example, the termination clause might reference the payment terms, so the relevant summary is passed forward when processing the termination clause.

3. **Summarization and Key Data Extraction**:
   - For the **Payment Terms** section, the key obligations are summarized:
     - "The client must pay within 30 days of receiving an invoice."
     - "A 5% late fee applies if payment is delayed."
     - "Service can be terminated if payments are overdue by more than 60 days."
   - The **Liability Limitations** section is similarly summarized:
     - "The provider is not liable for indirect damages."
     - "Total liability is capped at the fees paid by the client in the last 12 months."

4. **Optimization**:
   - **Dynamic Chunking** ensures that no individual section exceeds the token limit. For longer sections, like the liability clause, the text is split into smaller chunks, with overlaps to maintain continuity.
   - **Caching** is used for common phrases and standard clauses found in multiple sections, such as "The client shall..." or "Neither party is liable for..."

5. **Final Output**:

- ○ A full contract summary is provided to the legal team, highlighting key legal obligations, payment conditions, and potential risks, such as the strict liability limitations or the risk of early termination due to non-payment.

Result: The legal team receives a concise yet detailed summary of the contract, allowing them to quickly assess risks and advise their client without having to manually review the entire 50-page document. The optimized process ensures quick turnaround time and accurate, legally coherent analysis.

Example 2: Reviewing a Compliance Report with Over 100 Pages

In this scenario, a company is undergoing a compliance audit, and the auditors have produced a detailed report that is over 100 pages long. The report covers various areas of compliance, from data security to labor laws, with each section containing a mix of technical jargon, legalese, and compliance standards.

Scenario: The company's legal and compliance teams need a high-level summary of the report, with the ability to drill down into specific areas that may need immediate attention or carry higher risks.

Steps Taken:

1. **Document Segmentation and Prioritization**:
   - ○ The compliance report is segmented into major areas such as:
     - **Data Security**
     - **Labor Compliance**
     - **Environmental Regulations**
     - **Financial Reporting**

These sections are prioritized based on their relevance to the company's operations. For example, the **Data Security** section is flagged as a high priority due to recent regulatory changes.

1. **Focused Summarization**:
    - Each section is processed with specific instructions. For example, the **Labor Compliance** section is summarized with a focus on identifying any violations or non-compliance issues:
        - "The company is compliant with minimum wage regulations."
        - "A potential issue is flagged regarding overtime pay policies, which need further review."
    - For the **Data Security** section, the summarization includes key risks and recommendations:
        - "Data encryption standards meet regulatory requirements."
        - "The audit found that employee access controls need improvement to prevent unauthorized access."
    - The **Financial Reporting** section focuses on adherence to financial regulations:
        - "Financial statements were found to be accurate, with no discrepancies."
        - "Recommendations include improved documentation for tax-related expenses."
2. **Optimization Techniques**:
    - **Parallel Processing** is used to handle different sections simultaneously, significantly speeding up the process.
    - **Layered Summarization**: After the initial pass through each section, a second-layer summarization is applied to provide a more detailed breakdown of the most critical sections, such as labor compliance and data security.

3. **Performance Enhancements**:
    ◦ **Caching and Reuse**: The report includes repeated references to regulatory standards. Instead of reprocessing these, cached summaries of the relevant standards are used to reduce API calls.
    ◦ **Dynamic Chunking**: For longer sections, such as **Environmental Regulations**, where multiple compliance areas are covered, I split the text into smaller chunks, each focusing on a specific regulation (e.g., air quality, water usage).
4. **Final Output**:
    ◦ The compliance team receives an executive summary of the entire report, with detailed highlights on key areas of concern. Sections are categorized by risk level (e.g., high risk, medium risk, compliant) so the team can prioritize their follow-up actions.

Result: The company's legal and compliance teams are able to quickly identify areas that need immediate attention and take action, rather than sifting through the entire report. The use of layered summarization and prioritization ensures that high-risk areas are fully understood, while less critical sections receive lighter processing.

Example 3: Processing a Large Employment Agreement

Employment agreements are often lengthy and complex, with numerous clauses related to compensation, benefits, confidentiality, non-compete clauses, and termination terms. These agreements need to be reviewed thoroughly, as they can have significant legal implications.

Scenario: A business is negotiating employment agreements with senior executives and needs to understand key differences between the agreements, particularly focusing on compensation, non-compete clauses, and termination terms.

Steps Taken:

1. **Segmentation and Analysis**:
    - The employment agreements are divided into key sections:
        - **Compensation**
        - **Confidentiality**
        - **Non-Compete Clauses**
        - **Termination Terms**

Each section is processed individually, with detailed analysis applied to the non-compete clauses and termination terms.

1. **Key Data Extraction**:
    - For the **Compensation** section, the system extracts the core elements:
        - "Base salary: $200,000."
        - "Annual bonus: 20% of salary, based on performance."
    - For the **Non-Compete Clause**, the system highlights any restrictions:
        - "The employee agrees not to engage in competitive activities within the industry for a period of two years after termination."
2. **Chain-of-Thought Processing**:
    - Since the **Termination Terms** section references other parts of the agreement (e.g., non-compete and compensation), the system carries over relevant summaries to maintain continuity. For instance:
        - "Termination with cause results in forfeiture of the bonus."
        - "The non-compete clause remains in effect for two years after termination, regardless of cause."
    - This ensures that the analysis of termination terms

reflects the overall agreement.

3. **Final Output**:
    - The HR and legal teams receive a comparison of the employment agreements, with a focus on areas that could affect negotiations. For example:
        - Differences in compensation packages between executives are flagged.
        - The non-compete clauses are summarized and any variations between agreements are highlighted.
    - Potential risks, such as overly restrictive non-compete terms or unclear termination conditions, are flagged for further legal review.

Result: The business can quickly identify and negotiate key terms in the employment agreements, focusing on the most critical areas such as compensation and legal restrictions. The analysis helps ensure that both parties are clear on the terms, reducing the risk of disputes later on.

These practical examples illustrate how the techniques of segmentation, chain-of-thought processing, optimization, and summarization work together to handle complex, large-scale document processing tasks. By applying these methods, I was able to streamline workflows, reduce token consumption, and ensure high-quality outputs that met the needs of legal, compliance, and business teams.

Advanced Methods for Interfacing with the OpenAI API: Bringing Legal Document Analysis to Life

In this section, we will dive deeper into how I leveraged the OpenAI API for handling large-scale legal document analysis. We will explore the methods I used to efficiently manage token limits, integrate real-time processing, and create outputs that could be visualized or embedded into business workflows. Each method highlights the ways in which the

OpenAI API served as the backbone of an intelligent system, capable of breaking down complex legal language into digestible insights.

1. Token Management: Navigating the OpenAI API's Limits

At the core of any interaction with the OpenAI API is the concept of **token limits**. Each model has a maximum number of tokens that it can process in a single request, meaning both the input text and the output response must fit within that limit.

Challenge: Legal documents, especially contracts, can easily exceed these limits. A single agreement could range from 20,000 to 100,000 tokens in length.

Solution: I used **dynamic chunking**—breaking down the document into manageable sections, ensuring each chunk was processed with context from the previous sections. The method was a blend of automation and insight: automated tools broke the document into sections, while I introduced strategies like overlapping context to ensure the API maintained an understanding of the overall document flow.

How It Works:

- I first analyzed the document to identify **logical breakpoints** (e.g., by clause, section, or paragraph) rather than blindly cutting based on token count.
- **Overlap strategy**: The final few sentences from one chunk were repeated in the next to ensure continuity of context for the OpenAI API.
- Token-saving techniques: I streamlined input, ensuring only relevant text was sent to avoid wasting tokens on unnecessary boilerplate language.

Example Code for Token Calculation:

To predict token usage and manage chunk size, I used the OpenAI tokenizer to gauge how many tokens each section would use:

```python
python
Copy code
```

```
import openai
import tiktoken
def count_tokens(text, model="gpt-3.5-turbo"):
enc = tiktoken.encoding_for_model(model)
tokens = enc.encode(text)
return len(tokens)
document_text = "This is an example of a lengthy contract clause..."
token_count = count_tokens(document_text)
print(f"Number of tokens: {token_count}")
```

What Makes This Exciting? By intelligently chunking the text, I allowed the API to process contracts that would typically be "too large" for any single request. This innovation ensured that the analysis didn't lose coherence, even when handling extensive documents. Think of it like reading a book chapter by chapter, but always remembering what came before!

2. Chain-of-Thought Processing: Maintaining Coherence Across Sections

While breaking documents into smaller chunks is effective, the real magic happened with **chain-of-thought processing**. This method helped the OpenAI API "remember" previous chunks, ensuring that the insights from earlier sections fed into later ones.

Challenge: Contracts are inherently connected. For example, a termination clause might reference payment terms or liability caps discussed 30 pages earlier. Standard chunking alone would lose these references, and the AI could misinterpret the document.

Solution: I crafted a system where each chunk's output—whether a summary, key data points, or extracted risks—was fed back into subsequent API calls. This method allowed the AI to keep track of important connections between clauses and maintain an understanding of the entire document.

How It Works:

- **Inter-chunk context passing**: After each chunk was processed, the key points were extracted and re-sent as part of the next

API call's input, ensuring continuity.

- **Incremental prompts**: Instead of restarting from scratch with each chunk, the OpenAI API worked incrementally, building on its earlier analysis.

Example of a Chain-of-Thought Prompt:

Here's an example of how I structured a chain-of-thought prompt for contract analysis:

```python
Copy code
previous_summary = "The payment terms specify a 30-day window with penalties for late payments."
current_chunk = "The termination clause states that the contract can be terminated if payments are overdue by more than 60 days."
combined_input = f"Previous summary: {previous_summary}\n\nCurrent section: {current_chunk}"
response = openai.Completion.create(
model="gpt-4",
prompt=combined_input,
max_tokens=300
)
```

What Makes This Exciting? This method enabled the OpenAI API to work as if it were reading and understanding an entire document, even when processing it in pieces. It's like having an AI with perfect memory—allowing it to "understand" contracts holistically rather than in isolation.

3. Summarization as a Tool for Efficiency

When dealing with documents that stretched well beyond the token limit, **summarization** was the next natural step. Instead of analyzing every word in detail, I programmed the OpenAI API to summarize sections that were less critical, saving time and tokens while focusing on the most important clauses.

Challenge: Some legal sections—such as boilerplate confidentiality clauses or governing law statements—don't need deep analysis.

Processing these at the same level of detail as payment terms or liability clauses would be inefficient.

Solution: By instructing the API to summarize non-critical sections and save in-depth processing for key sections, I optimized both token usage and analysis speed.

How It Works:

- **Selective Summarization**: I identified which parts of the document required detailed analysis and which could be summarized. This selective approach allowed for a deeper dive into critical areas, such as indemnity clauses or non-compete agreements.

- **Layered Summarization**: For particularly long sections, I applied multiple layers of summarization—first summarizing the entire section, then diving deeper into specific paragraphs or sentences flagged as high priority.

Example Prompt for Summarization:

```python
Copy code
document_section = "The governing law for this agreement shall be the laws of Ontario..."
response = openai.Completion.create(
model="gpt-4",
prompt=f"Summarize the following legal section: {document_section}",
max_tokens=100
)
summary = response.choices[0].text.strip()
print(f"Summary: {summary}")
```

What Makes This Exciting? Summarization allowed me to handle large documents with agility, preserving resources for the sections that mattered most. It's like skipping the filler in a novel to get straight to the action!

4. Real-Time Data Extraction for Decision Making

Another powerful use of the OpenAI API was real-time **data extraction**. Legal teams often want specific answers without wading through entire documents. For example, they might need to know key dates, financial obligations, or termination conditions.

Challenge: Legal contracts can hide critical information deep within complex clauses. Finding that information manually is tedious and prone to errors.

Solution: I used the OpenAI API to extract key data in real-time, such as:

- Dates of obligation (e.g., deadlines, start dates, renewal dates).
- Financial terms (e.g., penalties, payment schedules).
- Risk-related clauses (e.g., liability caps, termination conditions).

How It Works:

- **Targeted Queries**: Instead of analyzing every part of the document equally, I asked specific questions of the API, focusing only on the key data needed. This reduced token usage while delivering precise information.
- **Custom Prompts**: Each prompt was tailored to extract a specific type of information (e.g., financial terms) without overloading the system with unnecessary context.

Example of Real-Time Data Extraction:

```python
python
Copy code
document_text = "The service provider shall be paid within 30 days, with a 5% penalty for late payments."
query = "What is the payment schedule and penalty for late payments in this contract?"
response = openai.Completion.create(
model="gpt-4",
```

```
prompt=f"{document_text}\n\n{query}",
max_tokens=100
)
extracted_info = response.choices[0].text.strip()
print(f"Extracted Info: {extracted_info}")
```

What Makes This Exciting? Imagine being able to pull out crucial legal terms or obligations in seconds—without having to read through dense legalese. This method turned document analysis into an on-demand query system, making it fast and accurate for business decisions.

---

5. Visualization of Data with API Outputs

Finally, to take the API's output a step further, I integrated real-time **data visualization** directly into the analysis pipeline. For example, once the API identified risks or summarized terms, I could use these outputs to create charts that made the data more digestible.

Challenge: Text-based summaries are great, but visuals can often tell the story more clearly, especially when presenting data to stakeholders.

Solution: After the OpenAI API performed its analysis, I generated charts—like bar charts showing the frequency of key terms, pie charts displaying risk breakdowns, or timelines of contract deadlines—to offer visual insights alongside textual analysis.

How It Works:

- **Output Parsing**: The API's outputs (summaries, data points, risks) were formatted into structured data, which was then passed into a charting library (like matplotlib in Python).
- **Automatic Visualization**: Once the API identified key terms or clauses, I created visual representations of this data (e.g., showing how often "penalty," "liability," or "termination" appeared across a document).

Example of API-Driven Visualization:

Let's say the API identifies key legal terms and their frequencies:

```
python
Copy code
import matplotlib.pyplot as plt
terms = ['Penalty', 'Termination', 'Liability', 'Payment']
frequency = [5, 7, 10, 8]
plt.bar(terms, frequency, color='blue')
plt.xlabel('Terms')
plt.ylabel('Frequency')
plt.title('Key Legal Terms in Contract')
plt.show()
```

What Makes This Exciting? Imagine running a contract through an AI and instantly seeing a visual breakdown of its most critical terms—without having to manually sift through the document. It's like having a dashboard for legal analysis!

Conclusion: The Power of the OpenAI API in Legal Document Processing

By harnessing the OpenAI API with methods like dynamic chunking, chain-of-thought processing, selective summarization, and real-time data extraction, I turned what could have been a complex, time-consuming task into a streamlined and efficient process. These tools allowed me to not only handle documents of massive size but also to distill critical insights, automate tedious tasks, and present findings in a way that was both actionable and easy to understand.

For readers delving into AI-driven document processing, the key takeaway is that the OpenAI API isn't just a tool for text generation—it's a bridge to deeper, more intelligent analysis, capable of turning dense contracts into actionable insights with speed and accuracy. The combination of smart interfacing methods, efficiency optimizations, and visual storytelling transforms how we interact with complex legal documents, paving the way for more dynamic and responsive workflows in the legal and business worlds.

Handling Retries in OpenAI API: Ensuring Robust and Reliable Document Processing

When interfacing with the OpenAI API, especially for complex tasks like large document processing or legal analysis, it's critical to have a robust system to handle **retries**. API requests can fail for a variety of reasons—rate limits, timeouts, token overflows, or temporary connectivity issues. Designing an effective retry strategy ensures that these failures don't halt the document analysis process, and that the system gracefully recovers and continues working.

In this section, I'll describe the methods I used to handle retries, mitigate errors, and optimize performance for a seamless experience when working with the OpenAI API.

Why Retries Are Essential

Challenge: API failures can occur for several reasons:

1. **Rate Limiting**: OpenAI imposes limits on how many requests you can send per minute.
2. **Timeouts**: Sometimes, the request can take longer than expected and time out.
3. **Token Overflows**: Sending too many tokens in one request can cause errors.
4. **Network Issues**: Temporary connectivity issues or server unavailability can cause failures.

Solution: Implementing a retry strategy ensures that these transient issues don't cause the entire document processing workflow to fail. Instead of crashing, the system waits, retries the request, and if necessary, modifies the request to meet API limits (e.g., reducing the token count).

Key Strategies for Handling Retries

1. **Exponential Backoff**: This method ensures that the system waits progressively longer between retries, reducing the load on the API while giving enough time for issues like rate limiting to resolve.
2. **Token Overflow Handling**: If a request exceeds the token

limit, it's essential to have an automated fallback that reduces the input size, re-chunks the document, and retries the request.

3. **Error Categorization**: Not all errors are equal. Some can be retried (like rate limits), while others indicate more serious issues (like invalid API keys). Classifying errors ensures that the system only retries when appropriate.

4. **Graceful Degradation**: In the event of persistent failures, the system can degrade gracefully—falling back to a simpler mode (e.g., lighter summarization instead of full document analysis) rather than crashing completely.

Method 1: Exponential Backoff for Retry

Exponential Backoff is the most commonly used retry strategy when dealing with API rate limits or timeouts. The idea is to progressively increase the delay between retries, allowing temporary issues to resolve while avoiding overloading the system.

How It Works:

- **First Retry**: Wait a short amount of time (e.g., 1 second) before retrying.
- **Second Retry**: Wait longer (e.g., 2 seconds).
- **Subsequent Retries**: Keep doubling the wait time until a maximum limit is reached (e.g., 16 seconds).

Example of Exponential Backoff in Python:

```python
python
Copy code
import time
import openai
def retry_with_exponential_backoff(prompt, model="gpt-4", max_retries=5):
    retries = 0
    backoff = 1 # Start with 1 second delay
    while retries < max_retries:
        try:
```

```python
response = openai.Completion.create(
model=model,
prompt=prompt,
max_tokens=150
)
return response.choices[0].text.strip()
except openai.error.RateLimitError as e:
retries += 1
print(f"Rate limit exceeded. Retrying in {backoff} seconds...")
time.sleep(backoff)
backoff *= 2 # Double the wait time after each retry
except openai.error.Timeout as e:
retries += 1
print(f"Request timed out. Retrying in {backoff} seconds...")
time.sleep(backoff)
backoff *= 2
except openai.error.APIError as e:
print(f"API error occurred: {e}. Retrying...")
retries += 1
time.sleep(backoff)
backoff *= 2
# If all retries fail
raise Exception("Max retries reached. The API is currently unavailable.")
```

What Makes This Effective?

- **Progressive Delay**: By gradually increasing the wait time, this strategy allows temporary problems (like rate limiting or timeouts) to resolve themselves without overwhelming the API with repeated requests.
- **Retry Limit**: Setting a maximum retry limit prevents infinite loops in case of a persistent failure.

Method 2: Token Overflow Handling

When working with large documents, exceeding the API's token limit is a common issue. Instead of simply failing, the system can be designed to detect token overflows, adjust the input size, and retry the request.

How It Works:

- Before sending a request, the system calculates the token count of the input.
- If the token count exceeds the limit (e.g., 4096 tokens for GPT-3 or 8192 tokens for GPT-4), the system automatically **chunks the input** and retries the request with a smaller chunk size.

Example of Handling Token Overflow:

```python
python
Copy code
import openai
import tiktoken
def chunk_input_if_necessary(prompt, max_tokens_allowed=4096, model="gpt-3.5-turbo"):
    enc = tiktoken.encoding_for_model(model)
    tokens = enc.encode(prompt)
    # If the token count exceeds the allowed limit, chunk the input
    if len(tokens) > max_tokens_allowed:
        # Reduce the input size and retry
        chunked_prompt = prompt[:max_tokens_allowed-100] # Ensure enough space for the output tokens
        print(f"Input exceeds token limit. Chunking to {max_tokens_allowed-100} tokens.")
        return chunked_prompt
    else:
        return prompt
def call_openai_with_retries(prompt, model="gpt-3.5-turbo"):
    # Prepare the input prompt
    processed_prompt = chunk_input_if_necessary(prompt)
    # Make the API call
    response = openai.Completion.create(
        model=model,
        prompt=processed_prompt,
```

```
max_tokens=150 # For the output
)
return response.choices[0].text.strip()
```

What Makes This Effective?

- **Automatic Chunking**: This system anticipates token overflows, reducing the input size automatically, so the request can still be processed without manual intervention.
- **Retry with Reduced Input**: The system doesn't give up after the first failure. Instead, it dynamically adjusts the request to fit within the token limit, ensuring that critical sections are still processed.

Method 3: Error Categorization and Custom Handling

Not all errors are created equal. By categorizing errors, the system can handle each one in the most appropriate way. For example:

- **RateLimitError**: Retry after a delay.
- **InvalidRequestError**: Likely due to an issue with the input. This error shouldn't trigger a retry without modifying the request.
- **APIError**: Retry with exponential backoff.
- **TimeoutError**: Retry after a delay.

Example of Error Categorization and Handling:

```python
python
Copy code
import openai
import time
def api_request_with_error_handling(prompt, model="gpt-4", max_retries=5):
retries = 0
while retries < max_retries:
try:
response = openai.Completion.create(
```

```python
        model=model,
        prompt=prompt,
        max_tokens=300
    )
    return response.choices[0].text.strip()
except openai.error.RateLimitError:
    print("Rate limit reached. Retrying...")
    time.sleep(2 ** retries)
    retries += 1
except openai.error.InvalidRequestError:
    print("Invalid request. Check your input.")
    return "Invalid request. Please adjust your input."
except openai.error.APIError:
    print("API error occurred. Retrying...")
    time.sleep(2 ** retries)
    retries += 1
except openai.error.Timeout:
    print("Request timed out. Retrying...")
    time.sleep(2 ** retries)
    retries += 1
return "Request failed after multiple retries."
```

What Makes This Effective?

- **Error-Specific Handling**: Different errors trigger different actions, allowing the system to intelligently respond to issues rather than blindly retrying the same request.
- **Custom Responses**: For unrecoverable errors (like InvalidRequestError), the system can provide immediate feedback without wasting retries.

Method 4: Graceful Degradation

If all retries fail, it's important that the system doesn't simply give up. Instead, I implemented a **graceful degradation** mechanism, which ensured that if a complex task couldn't be completed, a simpler version would still be returned.

How It Works:

- **Fallback to Summarization**: If the system can't process the full document, it falls back to summarizing key sections rather than performing a detailed analysis.
- **Partial Processing**: If token limits or errors prevent full document processing, the system outputs a partial summary of the sections that were successfully processed.

Example of Graceful Degradation:

```python
python
Copy code
def fallback_to_summarization(text):
# If detailed processing fails, return a simple summary
summary_prompt = f"Summarize the following: {text}"
response = openai.Completion.create(
model="gpt-3.5-turbo",
prompt=summary_prompt,
max_tokens=100
)
return response.choices[0].text.strip()
def process_document_with_fallback(document_text):
try:
```

When you incorporated the "Chain of Thought" (CoT) reasoning into your OpenAI API Contract Analysis program, you used a highly effective and logical technique to break down complex contract elements into manageable, interpretable steps. Chain of Thought refers to the structured and sequential reasoning process that models follow to reach conclusions, mirroring the way humans think through complex problems. By guiding the AI through a clear thought process, CoT allows it to process intricate tasks with higher accuracy and produce more coherent, logically consistent outputs.

The Power of Chain of Thought:

1. **Improves Comprehension and Depth**: CoT enables the AI to

process the task step by step, which is especially crucial in legal contract analysis where multiple layers of interpretation are required. Instead of generating a response all at once, the AI is prompted to reason through each clause, term, or concept independently, thus improving the depth of its analysis.

2. **Encourages Detailed Explanations**: Chain of Thought reasoning pushes the model to explain why it arrives at certain conclusions. This is particularly useful when identifying potential issues in contracts such as ambiguous language, unfair terms, or conflicting clauses. By forcing the model to articulate its reasoning, it can spot nuances that might otherwise be missed if it were just attempting to give a "quick answer."

3. **Enhances Decision-Making**: In contract analysis, identifying risks or points of negotiation requires a systematic approach. CoT allows the model to evaluate each section of the contract logically, mapping out its decision-making process. This ensures that the AI does not overlook critical aspects such as liability limits, termination clauses, or dispute resolution mechanisms.

The Interesting Method You Used:

Your approach involved **embedding the CoT process into a multi-layered prompt structure**, which guided the AI through a logical breakdown of the contract's components. This method is particularly innovative because it mirrors how a human expert would analyze a contract—starting with high-level categories (e.g., liability, payment terms, termination clauses) and then drilling down into specific elements within each category.

Step-by-Step Breakdown:

1. **Initial High-Level Categorization**: You prompted the AI to categorize the contract into distinct sections, such as

'Liabilities,' 'Rights and Responsibilities,' 'Termination Clauses,' etc. This high-level organization helped the AI focus its attention on specific domains without getting lost in the complexity of the entire document.

2. **Layered Thought Process within Each Category**: Within each category, the AI was prompted to break down key clauses, explain their intent, and explore any potential risks or ambiguities. For example, if analyzing a 'Termination Clause,' the AI might be prompted to first explain what triggers termination, then explore whether there are penalties, and finally assess whether the conditions for termination are balanced or biased towards one party.

3. **Cross-Referencing Clauses**: One of the more innovative aspects of your method was prompting the AI to **cross-reference clauses** to look for contradictions. For example, if a termination clause contradicts a confidentiality clause (as can often happen in contracts), the AI could flag this as a risk area. This ensures the analysis is not siloed but rather holistic, taking into account the full scope of the contract.

4. **Iterative Reasoning for Ambiguities**: Instead of accepting ambiguity at face value, your program instructed the AI to propose multiple interpretations for vague language. For example, if a clause used vague terms like "reasonable" or "significant," the AI, guided by CoT, would propose different scenarios under which those terms might be interpreted, and then weigh the implications of each. This iterative approach improves the robustness of the analysis.

The Importance of Using Chain of Thought for Better Results:
By using CoT in contract analysis, you effectively simulate a more **human-like reasoning process** within the AI, which is critical when interpreting something as nuanced as legal language. Contracts often

require analysis that is not just syntactical but contextual—reading between the lines and understanding the intent behind the words. CoT allows the AI to apply this more advanced reasoning model, resulting in:

- **Improved detection of risks and ambiguities** that would otherwise be missed by simple keyword or phrase analysis.
- **Better alignment with human legal reasoning**, making it easier for lawyers and contract managers to trust and adopt AI-generated insights.
- **More actionable feedback** for contract negotiation, as the AI is not just identifying issues but explaining the logic behind them, making it easier to adjust clauses or address identified risks.

In summary, your use of Chain of Thought reasoning transforms the AI from a tool that passively interprets legal texts into an active analytical engine, capable of producing detailed, well-reasoned insights. This makes the contract analysis process far more reliable, accurate, and thorough, setting your program apart from simpler AI-driven contract review systems that lack this level of cognitive sophistication.

The Benefits of Chain of Thought

Chain of Thought (CoT) reasoning brings several key benefits to AI-based applications, particularly those that deal with complex, multi-step tasks like contract analysis, problem-solving, and reasoning-based outputs. Here's a detailed breakdown of the primary benefits of using Chain of Thought:

1. Enhanced Comprehension and Contextual Understanding

- **Step-by-Step Reasoning**: CoT helps the AI think through a problem or task in a structured manner, ensuring it doesn't skip over important details or make hasty conclusions. This is particularly useful in tasks like contract analysis, where each clause or term may have far-reaching implications.

- **Deep Understanding of Complex Information**: Rather than providing surface-level answers, CoT helps the AI unpack the layers of complexity within the text, such as legal nuances or ambiguous language, resulting in more in-depth and meaningful insights.

2. Improved Accuracy and Logical Consistency

- **Reduction in Errors**: Since CoT forces the AI to follow a methodical path, it reduces the likelihood of errors caused by overlooking important details. For instance, when analyzing a legal contract, missing a key term or condition could lead to incorrect conclusions; CoT minimizes such risks by prompting detailed and logical examination at every step.

- **Maintaining Consistency**: By considering the entire context of a document or problem, CoT ensures that the output remains consistent across all parts. For instance, in contract analysis, the AI can ensure that terms are interpreted consistently throughout the document and that cross-references between clauses are logically aligned.

3. Better Handling of Ambiguities

- **Exploration of Multiple Interpretations**: Contracts and complex texts often contain ambiguous or vague language. CoT enables the AI to propose multiple possible interpretations rather than relying on a single, potentially incorrect reading. This exploration of ambiguity is critical in legal and technical documents where interpretations can have significant consequences.
- **Weighing Alternatives**: Once multiple interpretations are proposed, the AI can weigh the likelihood or consequences of each, helping users make more informed decisions when faced with unclear language.

4. Increased Transparency and Explainability

- **Rationale Behind Decisions**: One of the core benefits of CoT is that it encourages the AI to explain its reasoning in a clear, traceable way. This is crucial in tasks like legal contract analysis, where users need to understand not just the result but also the reasoning that led to that result. CoT allows the AI to articulate its thought process, making the analysis more transparent and explainable.
- **Trustworthiness**: AI systems that explain their decisions are generally more trusted by users, especially in fields like law, finance, and medicine, where the consequences of mistakes are high. With CoT, users can follow the AI's logic and assess whether it aligns with their expectations and understanding.

5. Handling Complex, Multi-Step Tasks

- **Decomposing Complex Problems**: CoT excels in tasks that require breaking down a large or complex problem into smaller, more manageable components. In contract analysis, for example, a contract can be broken down into sections (like liabilities, indemnifications, terms of service), and each section can be analyzed in detail before drawing conclusions about the entire contract.

- **Sequencing Actions**: For tasks that require logical progression, CoT helps ensure that the AI tackles each part of the task in the correct sequence. This methodical approach is especially useful when each step depends on the prior ones, ensuring that the AI's conclusions are well-founded and not prematurely reached.

6. Better Performance on Zero-Shot or Few-Shot Tasks

- **Minimal Training Data Requirements**: CoT reasoning often enhances the AI's performance even when the model has little or no specific training data for a given task (zero-shot or few-shot learning). This means that even in unfamiliar contexts, the AI can apply logical reasoning based on instructions or examples given in the prompt.

- **Generalization of Knowledge**: CoT enables the AI to apply knowledge more broadly, rather than relying on rote memorization of training data. This generalization capability allows the AI to perform more reliably across a wide range of situations, even those it has not seen before.

7. Creative and Complex Problem Solving

- **Generating Novel Insights**: In tasks where creative or outside-the-box thinking is required, CoT enables the AI to build on initial ideas, iterate through possibilities, and come up with novel solutions. This is especially relevant in contract analysis or negotiation, where standard clauses might need to be creatively modified to meet specific needs.
- **Exploring Hypotheticals**: CoT allows the AI to explore "what-if" scenarios effectively. In contract analysis, this could mean the AI not only flags risks but also suggests alternative clauses or wording to mitigate potential legal exposure.

8. Supporting User Decision-Making

- **Providing Actionable Recommendations**: Because CoT encourages the AI to think through problems logically, it is better equipped to offer actionable recommendations, not just surface-level insights. For example, in contract analysis, after identifying a problematic clause, the AI might recommend revisions or alternative wording based on its reasoning.
- **Empowering Non-Experts**: CoT can guide non-expert users through complex documents or problems by breaking them down into understandable components. This is highly beneficial in legal or technical fields, where users may not have deep expertise but need to make informed decisions.

Practical Example in Your Program:

In your OpenAI API Contract Analysis Program, you integrated CoT reasoning to ensure the AI approached each contract with the same rigor as a human expert might. For example, when analyzing a termination clause, the CoT approach would prompt the AI to:

1. Identify the conditions under which termination is allowed.

2. Consider any penalties or repercussions.
3. Cross-reference with other sections (e.g., confidentiality clauses or non-compete clauses) to see if termination triggers any conflicting conditions.
4. Weigh the implications of these clauses on both parties and suggest revisions if necessary.

This layered and thoughtful process is a direct result of CoT reasoning and leads to higher-quality contract analysis, as each step builds on the last, and the final output is more robust, accurate, and actionable.

In summary, the Chain of Thought approach makes AI systems like your contract analysis tool more **accurate**, **reliable**, **transparent**, and **capable of handling complex reasoning tasks**. It empowers users by providing deeper insights, clearer explanations, and more confidence in AI-generated outputs, making CoT an invaluable tool for developing sophisticated AI applications.

Section: Navigating Token Limits: Breaking Down Large Documents with OpenAI API

Handling token limitations is one of the most critical challenges when interfacing with the OpenAI API, especially when working with lengthy legal documents that can run well over the token cap. In this section, I'll explain the techniques I used to efficiently manage token limits, allowing me to analyze documents ranging from a few pages to hundreds, while maintaining a coherent flow of analysis.

The Challenge of Token Limits

OpenAI models, such as GPT-3 and GPT-4, have token limitations (e.g., 4096 or 8192 tokens, including both input and output). Legal documents often exceed this limit, especially complex contracts with multiple clauses and extensive terminology. So how can we work around these constraints while still preserving the integrity of the document?

Strategy: Document Segmentation

One of the first strategies I employed was **document segmentation**, where the document is broken down into smaller, logical parts for easier processing. The trick lies in splitting the document without losing context, which is essential in legal documents where different sections are deeply interconnected.

Key Steps:

1. **Logical Chunking**: I broke the document into natural divisions, like sections or clauses (e.g., Payment Terms, Termination Clauses). Each chunk was structured to fit within the token limit.
2. **Overlap Strategy**: I included small overlaps between chunks—typically repeating the last few sentences from one chunk at the start of the next—to ensure continuity.
3. **Contextual Prompts**: I used meta-information like section

headers (e.g., "Payment Terms") to give the AI context for each chunk, ensuring it understood the role of the text being processed.

Example:

```python
Copy code
def chunk_document(text, token_limit):
chunks = []
start = 0
while start < len(text):
end = min(len(text), start + token_limit - 100) # Reserving space for output
chunk = text[start:end]
chunks.append(chunk)
start = end - 50 # Overlap of 50 tokens to ensure continuity
return chunks
```

This method allowed me to process large documents piece by piece without losing the document's internal coherence.

Token-Saving Techniques

To further optimize token usage:

- **Summarize Before Processing**: I would pre-summarize verbose sections or legalese that didn't require detailed analysis, allowing me to focus on the sections that really mattered.
- **Selective Analysis**: By prioritizing critical sections, like "Liability Clauses" or "Payment Terms," I minimized the token load for less critical sections, improving both performance and relevance.

Section: Real-Time Data Extraction: Getting Specific Answers with the OpenAI API

One of the strengths of the OpenAI API is its ability to extract precise information from large documents in real time. For legal documents or contracts, there are often key details—such as specific dates, financial obligations, or clauses—that need to be pinpointed quickly without reading the entire document. I built my program around this concept, leveraging the OpenAI API to extract these critical data points dynamically.

The Challenge of Navigating Lengthy Documents

Imagine working through a contract that spans dozens of pages. Manually sifting through it to find key information like payment terms or non-compete clauses is time-consuming and prone to errors. Real-time data extraction with the OpenAI API simplifies this process by targeting specific information on-demand.

Strategy: Focused Queries for Targeted Results

Instead of processing an entire document in one go, I implemented **targeted queries** to zero in on specific pieces of information. For example, when analyzing a contract, I could ask the API to find details on payment schedules, penalty clauses, or liability caps, without having to process unrelated sections.

Key Steps:

1. **Targeted Prompts**: I crafted prompts to extract the exact information needed. For instance, if I wanted to know the **payment terms**, I would prompt the API to find only that section.
2. **Specific Extraction**: The API was directed to scan the document and pull relevant details like dates, amounts, or conditions from the text.
3. **Efficient Token Use**: By focusing only on key data points, the program used fewer tokens, allowing for more detailed responses within the token limit.

Example:
python
Copy code

```
document_text = "The service provider shall be paid within 30 days of submitting
an invoice. Failure to pay on time incurs a 5% penalty."
query = "What are the payment terms and late payment penalties?"
response = openai.Completion.create(
model="gpt-4",
prompt=f"{document_text}\n\n{query}",
max_tokens=100
)
extracted_info = response.choices[0].text.strip()
print(f"Extracted Info: {extracted_info}")
```

This method allowed me to **query documents like a database**, quickly extracting important details for review.

Application in Legal Review

In legal reviews, being able to extract data in real time—whether it's key clauses, dates, or obligations—greatly speeds up the process, ensuring nothing is missed. By using **real-time data extraction**, I was able to significantly enhance productivity, allowing legal teams to focus on higher-level decision-making rather than getting lost in the weeds.

Section: Error Handling and Retry Strategies: Ensuring Robust API Performance

While working with the OpenAI API, it's inevitable that you'll encounter errors or temporary issues such as rate limiting, timeouts, or even token overflow. To ensure that my program remained robust and didn't crash due to these transient issues, I implemented comprehensive **error handling** and **retry strategies**.

The Challenge: API Errors and Interruptions

The OpenAI API is powerful, but like any API, it can run into issues, particularly with high-demand tasks like processing large legal documents. Errors such as exceeding rate limits, request timeouts, or sending too many tokens can halt the workflow if not properly managed.

Strategy: Implementing Retry Mechanisms

To handle these issues, I designed the program with a retry mechanism that allowed it to recover from failures without requiring manual intervention. My approach involved:

1. **Exponential Backoff**: When an error occurred, the system would wait progressively longer between retries, giving the API time to recover.
2. **Error Categorization**: Not all errors are the same. I categorized errors into recoverable (e.g., rate limits or timeouts) and non-recoverable (e.g., invalid requests), and applied different retry strategies accordingly.
3. **Graceful Degradation**: If all retries failed, the system would fall back to a simpler mode, such as summarizing the document instead of performing a full analysis, ensuring that the user still received valuable output.

Example of a Retry Strategy:

```python
Copy code
import time
import openai
def retry_with_exponential_backoff(prompt, model="gpt-4", max_retries=5):
retries = 0
backoff = 1 # Start with 1 second delay
while retries < max_retries:
try:
response = openai.Completion.create(
model=model,
prompt=prompt,
max_tokens=200
)
return response.choices[0].text.strip()
except openai.error.RateLimitError:
retries += 1
print(f"Rate limit exceeded. Retrying in {backoff} seconds...")
time.sleep(backoff)
backoff *= 2 # Double the wait time after each retry
except openai.error.Timeout:
retries += 1
print(f"Request timed out. Retrying in {backoff} seconds...")
```

```
time.sleep(backoff)
backoff *= 2
    raise Exception("Max retries reached. API unavailable.")
```

Graceful Degradation: Handling Unrecoverable Errors

For persistent errors that couldn't be resolved after retries, the system didn't just fail outright. Instead, it **degraded gracefully** by switching to a more lightweight task—like summarizing the document instead of running a full analysis—ensuring that the user still received something of value.

Example of Graceful Degradation:

```python
Copy code
def fallback_to_summarization(document_text):
# If full analysis fails, return a simple summary
response = openai.Completion.create(
model="gpt-4",
prompt=f"Summarize the following document: {document_text}",
max_tokens=150
)
return response.choices[0].text.strip()
```

The Importance of Error Handling in Complex Workflows

Error handling and retry strategies are crucial for ensuring a smooth user experience. By designing the system to recover from errors automatically, I minimized downtime and improved reliability, making the program more robust when handling large-scale legal documents.

Section: Controlling Temperature and Fine-Tuning OpenAI's Responses

One of the fundamental aspects of interacting with the OpenAI API is controlling the **temperature** setting, which directly influences how creative or focused the responses from the model will be. When working on structured tasks, especially for legal document analysis, keeping responses precise and within acceptable bounds is critical.

What is Temperature?

The **temperature** parameter in the OpenAI API controls the randomness of the model's outputs. A lower temperature (e.g., 0 or 0.1) makes the model more deterministic and likely to produce accurate, structured responses. A higher temperature (e.g., 0.7 or 0.8) introduces more randomness, encouraging creative or diverse responses.

For tasks like legal document review or contract analysis, I favored **low temperature settings** to ensure that the model produced **fact-based, reliable answers**. Since legal documents demand high precision and adherence to existing clauses, creativity was less desirable than accuracy.

Example of Setting Temperature in a Prompt:

```python
Copy code
response = openai.Completion.create(
model="gpt-4",
prompt="Analyze the termination clause of this contract and highlight any risks.",
max_tokens=200,
temperature=0.2 # Lower temperature to ensure focused, fact-based response
)
```

Why Use Lower Temperatures in Legal Contexts?

By keeping the temperature low, I minimized the risk of the AI introducing unnecessary speculation or "hallucinations." This ensured that the responses were more focused on interpreting the document accurately, rather than providing imaginative interpretations.

Section: Crafting and Staging Super Prompts

A **superprompt** is a carefully designed input that maximizes the model's understanding of a task by guiding it with specific instructions and context. For large legal documents, I crafted superprompts to break down complex tasks, ensuring that each part of the analysis was thorough, accurate, and relevant.

The Importance of Super Prompts

Super prompts serve as a way to **stage** the processing of large documents, especially when there are different sections that need distinct levels of analysis. Each superprompt not only directs the model on how to interpret the content but also provides meta-instructions, guiding it through multiple steps of analysis.

Key Elements of a Super Prompt:

1. **Specific Instructions**: Super prompts are designed with precise instructions to ensure clarity. For example, instructing the model to focus on identifying risks in a liability clause rather than summarizing it.
2. **Contextual Information**: I included relevant context, such as earlier sections of the document or legal definitions, so the model had the information it needed to provide accurate results.
3. **Multiple Stages**: The superprompt would often be broken into **stages**, where the first prompt performs initial analysis, and the second prompt builds upon the first, extracting further insights or clarifying specific details.

Example of a Superprompt:

```python
Copy code
superprompt = """
1. Read the following Payment Terms section of the contract.
2. Summarize the key obligations for both parties.
3. Identify any potential risks, especially with regard to late payments or disputes.
4. Provide suggestions on how to mitigate these risks.
"""

response = openai.Completion.create(
model="gpt-4",
prompt=superprompt,
max_tokens=400,
temperature=0.3
)
```

This prompt carefully stages the tasks, asking the model first to understand the section, then summarize it, identify risks, and finally offer mitigation suggestions.

Staging Prompts for Complex Analysis

One of the methods I developed was breaking complex tasks into **staged prompts**:

- **Stage 1**: The model provides a high-level overview of the section (e.g., summarizing the payment terms).
- **Stage 2**: The next prompt asks the model to **dig deeper**, such as highlighting specific legal risks or ambiguities based on the initial summary.
- **Stage 3**: The final stage could involve asking the model to identify **potential conflicts** between the current section and other parts of the contract (e.g., how the termination clause interacts with payment terms).

By staging prompts, I ensured that the analysis built upon itself, delivering progressively deeper insights while keeping the process structured and focused.

Section: Data Cleansing: Preprocessing Legal Documents for OpenAI API

Before feeding a legal document or contract into the OpenAI API, **data cleansing** is an essential step. Legal documents often contain extraneous text (e.g., boilerplate language, redundant clauses, or irrelevant metadata), which can clutter the input and lead to inefficiencies in token usage. To optimize the document for analysis, I implemented several data cleansing techniques.

Key Data Cleansing Methods:

1. **Removing Boilerplate Text**: Sections like "Governing Law" or "Severability" that often don't require analysis were either

removed or summarized before sending to the API.

2. **Standardizing Terms**: Legal documents can use varying terminology. For example, "compensation" may also be referred to as "remuneration" or "payment." I standardized these terms to ensure consistency in the analysis.

3. **Eliminating Redundancies**: Legal contracts often contain repetitive clauses. I identified and eliminated repeated sections to prevent the model from wasting tokens on duplicate content.

4. **Filtering Irrelevant Sections**: Any parts of the document that were not legally significant (e.g., appendices or schedules) were filtered out before processing.

Example of Data Cleansing:

```python
Copy code
def clean_document(document_text):
# Remove boilerplate or redundant sections
cleaned_text = document_text.replace("This Agreement shall be governed by...", "")
# Standardize terminology
cleaned_text = cleaned_text.replace("remuneration", "payment")
# Remove any unnecessary metadata
return cleaned_text.strip()
cleaned_document = clean_document(document_text)
```

By cleaning the data before analysis, I reduced token usage and ensured that the model focused on the most critical sections of the document.

Section: Detecting and Preventing Hallucinations in OpenAI Responses

One challenge when working with AI models, especially in legal document analysis, is the risk of **hallucinations**—where the model generates information that isn't present in the input. In legal contexts, hallucinations can be particularly dangerous, as they may lead to incorrect interpretations or fabricated legal obligations.

The Challenge of Hallucinations

A hallucination occurs when the AI invents information or provides speculative answers that aren't supported by the document. This can happen if the model is prompted with incomplete context or asked open-ended questions that require factual data.

Strategy: Detecting and Preventing Hallucinations

To mitigate hallucinations, I implemented several techniques in my program:

1. **Low Temperature Settings**: Keeping the temperature low (0.1 to 0.3) helps ensure that the model sticks to the facts and avoids speculative responses.
2. **Fact-Checking Prompts**: I would re-prompt the model to fact-check its own responses. This involved feeding the generated response back into the system and asking it to verify the information based on the original document.
3. **Cross-Referencing Sections**: When analyzing a section, I often referenced other related sections to ensure that the AI didn't drift away from the actual content of the document.
4. **Explicit Boundaries**: In the prompt itself, I would explicitly instruct the model not to speculate or introduce new information that wasn't in the document.

Example of Hallucination Detection:

```python
python
Copy code
# First pass analysis
response = openai.Completion.create(
model="gpt-4",
prompt="Analyze the payment terms and provide key obligations for both parties.",
max_tokens=200,
temperature=0.2
)
# Fact-checking the response
```

```
fact_check_prompt = f"Based on the document, verify if the following obligations
are accurate: {response.choices[0].text.strip()}"
fact_check_response = openai.Completion.create(
model="gpt-4",
prompt=fact_check_prompt,
max_tokens=200,
temperature=0.2
)
```

By looping the AI's response back into itself for verification, I was able to detect and reduce hallucinations, ensuring that the final analysis was grounded in the actual content of the document.

Real-Time Corrections

In cases where hallucinations were detected, I had the system automatically issue corrections or flag the problematic section for human review. This way, the analysis didn't proceed with false information, maintaining the accuracy and reliability of the program's output.

Conclusion

By carefully managing model temperature, crafting staged superprompts, implementing data cleansing techniques, and detecting hallucinations, I built a robust system that allowed the OpenAI API to provide meaningful and accurate analysis of large legal documents. Each of these techniques plays a crucial role in ensuring that the program delivers precise, fact-based results, which are critical in legal contexts where accuracy is paramount.

Would you like to explore another technical section, such as **optimizing performance with parallel processing** or **creating detailed visualizations based on the API's output**? Let me know!

Below is a "cleaned" version of a super prompt I would use, noting these are not exact by merely replicas to illustrate the size and complexity of the super prompts I would use. Some super-prompts exceeded 5000 characters and at times 4 to 5 were used to generate the desired outcome I needed.

Super-Prompt Example 4: Comprehensive Contract Risk Assessment (Multi-Section)

Objective: Conduct a full-scale risk assessment across multiple sections of a contract, including Payment Terms, Liability Limitations, Confidentiality Agreements, and Termination Clauses. Identify key risks, ambiguities, and suggest revisions.

1. **Payment Terms Analysis**: Review the following Payment Terms section. Identify any obligations for both parties, including payment schedules, deadlines, and penalties for late payments. Highlight areas where the terms may be unclear, unfair, or expose either party to legal or financial risk.

2. **Liability Limitation Clause Review**: Examine the Liability Limitation clause. Specifically, identify the financial caps, types of liabilities excluded (e.g., indirect, consequential damages), and any ambiguities in the scope of the limitation. Assess whether the financial limits are reasonable given the nature of the contract, and identify any language that may expose one party to undue risk.

3. **Confidentiality Agreement Review**: Analyze the Confidentiality Agreement clause. Focus on identifying areas where the confidentiality obligations are overly broad, ambiguous, or potentially unenforceable. Assess whether the obligations extend beyond the scope of what is reasonable for the agreement, and whether exceptions to confidentiality are clearly defined.

4. **Termination Clause Assessment**: Review the Termination Clause and assess the conditions under which either party can terminate the contract. Identify potential conflicts between the termination conditions and other sections of the contract, such as payment terms or confidentiality. Highlight any risks associated with early termination, such as penalties or loss of service, and determine whether these penalties are clearly outlined and enforceable.

5. **Cross-Section Risk Detection**: Detect any potential conflicts between these sections (e.g., how the Liability Limitation clause affects obligations under the Payment

Terms or Termination Clause). Identify any risks or ambiguities that arise from overlapping terms or unclear dependencies between these sections. For instance, if the Liability Limitation contradicts the penalties under the Payment Terms, highlight this conflict.

6. **Mitigation Strategies and Revision Suggestions**: For each of the sections reviewed, provide suggestions for mitigating risks. This could include revising the language to clarify ambiguous terms, renegotiating financial limits, or redefining the scope of confidentiality obligations. Suggest alternative phrasing or additional clauses to better protect both parties and ensure the contract is enforceable in a legal context.

7. **Summarize Findings**: In two distinct sections:

a. List of key risks identified in each section (Payment Terms, Liability, Confidentiality, Termination).

b. Proposed revisions or amendments to reduce the risk and improve clarity in the contract.

Document Sections:

1. Payment Terms:

"[Insert Payment Terms Clause]"

2. Liability Limitation:

"[Insert Liability Limitation Clause]"

3. Confidentiality Agreement:

"[Insert Confidentiality Clause]"

4. Termination Clause:

"[Insert Termination Clause]"

Ensure that each part of the analysis is structured and well-organized. Each section should be analyzed independently before considering cross-references.

Purpose:

This super-prompt is designed for **comprehensive analysis**, guiding the model through several critical sections of a contract. The length and multi-step structure allow the model to handle each section methodically, ensuring depth and precision while maintaining the ability to detect cross-referenced risks across different clauses.

Super-Prompt Example 5: Legal Dispute Potential and Resolution Strategy (Advanced)

Objective: Identify potential points of dispute in a multi-party contract and suggest resolution strategies based on dispute resolution clauses, governing law, and liability limitations.

1. **Dispute Identification**: Begin by reviewing the following sections of the contract: Payment Terms, Governing Law, and Dispute Resolution Clause. Identify any areas of potential dispute between the parties involved. Focus particularly on clauses where terms are ambiguous, open to multiple interpretations, or where obligations may conflict.

2. **Governing Law and Jurisdiction**: Analyze the Governing Law section to determine which jurisdiction's laws apply in the event of a dispute. Identify any potential issues with the jurisdiction, such as conflicting laws in different regions or countries, and determine if the jurisdiction specified is advantageous to one party over the other. Highlight any areas where the governing law may conflict with the laws of a jurisdiction where the contract is being enforced.

3. **Dispute Resolution Clause**: Review the Dispute Resolution Clause in detail. Determine whether it specifies mediation, arbitration, or litigation, and evaluate the process outlined for resolving disputes. Identify any potential weaknesses in the dispute resolution process, such as vague timelines, unclear authority for the arbitrator or mediator, or a lack of enforcement mechanisms. Highlight any risks or burdens associated with the resolution method chosen.

4. **Liability Limitation Clause**: Cross-reference the Liability Limitation Clause with the Dispute Resolution Clause. Identify any conflicts between the financial limitations imposed by the Liability Limitation and the potential costs of resolving disputes. For example, if the liability cap is set lower than the potential cost of legal fees, highlight this as a risk.

5. **Early Termination and Penalties**: Assess the potential for disputes arising from early termination, particularly focusing on penalties or compensation clauses. Review any conditions under which either party may terminate the agreement and whether such conditions could lead to disputes regarding compensation, service delivery, or penalties.

6. **Risk Assessment and Dispute Likelihood**: Provide an overall assessment of the likelihood of disputes arising under this contract, focusing on the sections mentioned above. Determine which clauses are most likely to trigger legal conflicts and provide a ranking of high-risk areas.

7. **Suggested Amendments for Dispute Avoidance**: Suggest specific amendments to the contract that could help avoid disputes. This might include clarifying ambiguous terms, adjusting the governing law, or strengthening the dispute resolution process (e.g., specifying binding arbitration rather than non-binding mediation).

8. **Final Summary of Findings**:

a. Identified high-risk areas for potential disputes.

b. Recommended changes to avoid or mitigate the likelihood of disputes.

Document Sections:
1. Payment Terms:
"[Insert Payment Terms Clause]"
2. Governing Law:
"[Insert Governing Law Clause]"
3. Dispute Resolution:
"[Insert Dispute Resolution Clause]"
4. Liability Limitation:
"[Insert Liability Limitation Clause]"
5. Termination and Penalty Clauses:
"[Insert Termination and Penalty Clauses]"
Ensure the output is organized by section with clear distinctions between risks, conflicts, and recommended changes.

Purpose:

This super-prompt is designed for a **multi-layered legal risk and dispute potential analysis**. By integrating cross-references between clauses (like Governing Law, Liability Limitation, and Dispute Resolution), the model is guided to detect potential conflicts that could lead to legal disputes. It also sets up a structured process for assessing risks and suggesting actionable solutions.

Super-Prompt Example 6: Multi-Party Contract Clause Harmonization

Objective: Harmonize overlapping or conflicting clauses in a multi-party contract, focusing on non-compete agreements, confidentiality clauses, and service-level obligations.

1. **Non-Compete Clause Review**: Review the Non-Compete Clause provided below. Summarize the key restrictions placed on each party, including the scope, geographic limitations, and time period. Identify any areas where the non-compete obligations may conflict with other sections of the contract, particularly those related to service delivery or intellectual property.

2. **Confidentiality Clause Review**: Analyze the Confidentiality Clause to determine the scope of confidentiality obligations, exceptions to confidentiality, and the duration of the agreement. Identify any overlap with the Non-Compete Clause, especially where confidentiality restrictions may impact a party's ability to comply with non-compete obligations. Determine if the confidentiality terms are reasonable and enforceable.

3. **Service-Level Agreement (SLA) Assessment**: Review the Service-Level Agreement (SLA) section. Identify any obligations for service delivery, performance standards, or penalties for non-compliance. Cross-reference the SLA with the Non-Compete and Confidentiality Clauses, looking for any areas where obligations may conflict, such as intellectual property usage or delivery timelines impacted by non-compete restrictions.

4. **Conflict Detection**: Identify any conflicts between the Non-Compete, Confidentiality, and Service-Level Clauses. For example, if a party is required to provide certain services but is restricted by non-compete obligations or confidentiality terms, highlight this conflict. Provide an assessment of how these conflicts might impact the enforceability of the contract and whether they could lead to performance disputes.

5. **Proposed Revisions and Harmonization Strategies**: Suggest specific revisions to harmonize these clauses. This could include redefining the scope of non-compete obligations to avoid conflicts with the SLA, or adjusting confidentiality terms to allow for service compliance without breaching non-compete restrictions. Provide alternative phrasing or additional clauses to ensure all obligations are compatible and enforceable.

6. **Risk Summary**: Summarize the potential risks associated with the identified conflicts and recommend changes to mitigate these risks. Prioritize the sections where revisions are most critical.

7. **Final Recommendations**:

a. List of conflicts between Non-Compete, Confidentiality, and SLA sections.

b. Suggested harmonization strategies and specific language changes for each conflicting clause.

Document Sections:

1. Non-Compete Clause:

"[Insert Non-Compete Clause]"

2. Confidentiality Clause:

"[Insert Confidentiality Clause]"

3. Service-Level Agreement (SLA):

"[Insert

At the time of this writing, optimizing costs when using OpenAI API. The OpenAI API provides powerful natural language processing capabilities, but costs can add up quickly for large-scale document analysis. Whether you're working with legal contracts, financial reports, or other text-heavy documents, implementing cost optimization strategies is crucial. This article explores several approaches to reduce API expenses while still leveraging the power of models like GPT-4.

Why Cost Optimization Matters

OpenAI's pricing is based on the number of tokens processed. For context, 1,000 tokens is approximately 750 words. While this may seem small for individual queries, the costs can escalate rapidly when analyzing multiple lengthy documents. Let's look at the current pricing for OpenAI's most popular models:

- GPT-3.5-Turbo: $0.002 per 1K tokens (input + output)
- GPT-4: $0.03 per 1K tokens (input), $0.06 per 1K tokens (output)

A 10-page legal contract could easily contain 5,000 tokens. Processing 100 such documents daily with GPT-4 would cost around $150 per day just for the input tokens. Clearly, optimizing API usage can lead to significant savings.

Strategies for Cost Reduction

1. Use Summarization Techniques

Instead of processing entire documents, use summarization to extract key information first. This can be done using GPT-3.5-Turbo to create concise summaries, which can then be analyzed further with GPT-4 if needed. This two-step approach can dramatically reduce the number of tokens processed by the more expensive model.

1. Minimize Redundant API Calls

Avoid making repeated API calls for similar information. Cache responses when possible and implement proper error handling to prevent unnecessary retries. Additionally, batch similar queries together to reduce the overhead of multiple API requests.

1. Leverage GPT-3.5 for Simpler Tasks

While GPT-4 offers superior capabilities, it comes at a higher cost. Identify sections of your workflow that can be handled effectively by GPT-3.5-Turbo. For example, use GPT-3.5 for initial document classification or extracting basic metadata, reserving GPT-4 for more complex analysis.

1. Preprocess Documents

Before sending text to the API, preprocess your documents to remove non-essential content. This may include:

- Stripping out formatting and markup
- Removing boilerplate text or headers/footers
- Eliminating redundant sections

By reducing the input token count, you can significantly lower costs, especially when using GPT-4.

1. Implement Chunking Strategies

For very large documents, implement a chunking strategy. Break the document into smaller sections and process them individually. This allows for more granular control over which parts of the document require deeper analysis.

1. Fine-tune Custom Models

For specialized tasks that you perform frequently, consider fine-tuning a custom model. While there is an upfront cost, a fine-tuned model can often perform specific tasks more efficiently, requiring fewer tokens and potentially using a less expensive base model.

1. Monitor and Analyze Usage

Implement robust logging and analytics to track your API usage. This will help you identify areas of high token consumption and opportunities for optimization. OpenAI provides usage data, but supplementing this with your own tracking can provide deeper insights.

1. Set Token Limits

Implement hard limits on the number of tokens processed for each API call. This prevents unexpected cost spikes from extremely long inputs or outputs. Be sure to handle cases where the limit is reached gracefully in your application.

By implementing these strategies, you can significantly reduce your OpenAI API costs without sacrificing the power of advanced language models. Regular audits of your API usage and ongoing optimization efforts will ensure you're getting the most value from the OpenAI platform while keeping expenses in check. Remember, even small optimizations can lead to substantial savings when dealing with large-scale document processing.

Dealing with Complex Clauses and Edge Cases in Legal Documents

Why It's Important

Legal documents often contain highly complex or unusual clauses that can be challenging for even sophisticated AI models to interpret correctly. These complexities arise due to the use of vague terms, overlapping conditions, or intricate legal jargon, which can lead to ambiguous interpretations. Effectively handling these cases is crucial because they may expose the parties involved to risks, misinterpretation, or even legal disputes.

Approach in the Code

In your source code, you recognized the limitations of standard AI models when dealing with complex legal clauses. You developed methods to **highlight ambiguous language**, identify **conflicting clauses**, and **segment documents** to manage edge cases better.

1. Handling Ambiguous Language:

Your code included a feature that scans for specific ambiguous terms or phrases commonly found in legal documents (e.g., "reasonable efforts," "material adverse change," "subject to approval"). These terms often require additional scrutiny due to their inherent vagueness. Once detected, you used the OpenAI API to **generate explanations** for why certain phrases might lead to misinterpretations and provided recommendations for more precise language.

Here's an example snippet from your code:

```vb
Copy code
LG = Array("time to time", "reasonable efforts", "material adverse change", "force majeure", "good faith", ...)
If          docRange.Find.Execute(FindText:=LG(i),          Forward:=True, Wrap:=wdFindStop) Then
    ' Highlight the ambiguous term
    docRange.Shading.BackgroundPatternColor = RGB(0, 128, 128)
    docRange.Font.ColorIndex = wdWhite
    ' Prompt OpenAI to explain why the term is ambiguous
```

End If

2. Cross-Referencing Clauses to Detect Conflicts:

Many legal documents contain clauses that refer to other parts of the contract, such as termination clauses that might reference liability or confidentiality. You developed an approach where the API **cross-referenced sections** to detect potential conflicts between these interrelated clauses. For instance, if a termination clause contradicted the liability clause, the API would flag this issue, allowing you to make revisions.

```vb
Copy code
' Example of cross-referencing payment terms with liability clauses
If InStr(ClauseText, "payment terms") > 0 And InStr(OtherClauseText, "liability") > 0 Then
' Highlight potential conflicts between clauses
End If
```

3. Segmenting Complex Documents:

Given the length and complexity of some contracts, you implemented document segmentation. This allowed you to process chunks of text while maintaining context across segments. You leveraged chain-of-thought techniques to ensure that **previously analyzed sections** informed the interpretation of subsequent sections. For example, the analysis of payment terms would be carried over to the liability section to ensure consistency.

```vb
Copy code
' Break document into manageable chunks
For PageNumber = 1 To PageCount
CurrentPageText = GetPageText(PageNumber)
' Process each section while carrying context from previous sections
response = CallOpenAI(CurrentPageText, PreviousContext)
Next PageNumber
```

Lessons Learned and Adjustments

Throughout the process, you encountered several **edge cases** where the model either struggled with overly complex phrasing or generated responses that were too speculative. Here's how you addressed these issues:

1. **Adjusting Prompting for Complex Clauses**: By providing **more structured prompts**, you guided the model to focus on specific legal elements, reducing ambiguity in its responses. For example, rather than asking for a general analysis of a liability clause, you structured the prompt to explicitly highlight financial caps, liability exclusions, and the scope of liability.

2. **Refining Temperature Settings**: To prevent overly speculative responses, especially in highly sensitive legal areas, you reduced the temperature parameter of the API, ensuring that the responses remained **fact-based and focused**.

3. **Using Multi-Pass Verification**: In cases where the API's initial response was unclear or speculative, you implemented a **multi-pass verification process**. This involved feeding the response back into the model for re-verification, using explicit instructions to **correct potential errors** or inconsistencies.

```vb
Copy code
' Multi-pass verification to check for accuracy in responses
response = CallOpenAI(FirstPassResponse)
FactCheckResponse = CallOpenAI(VerifyResponse(FirstPassResponse))
```

Examples of Edge Cases

- **Force Majeure Clauses**: These clauses often contain a wide range of interpretations depending on jurisdiction and context. Your program specifically flagged vague terms like "acts of God" and provided alternative wording to clarify the scope of these clauses.

- **Termination Clauses**: The interplay between termination, liability, and confidentiality was often tricky. By cross-referencing sections, your program flagged conflicts where a termination could trigger an unintended confidentiality breach, providing a recommendation for rewording.

Conclusion

By implementing these strategies, you addressed some of the most challenging aspects of legal document analysis with the OpenAI API. The combination of **highlighting ambiguous terms, cross-referencing clauses**, and **segmenting documents** allowed for more precise and reliable interpretations, reducing the risk of misinterpretation and helping users navigate complex legal landscapes with confidence.

Closing Section: Bringing It All Together

As we conclude this journey through the intricate process of using the OpenAI API for legal document analysis, I hope you now have a deeper understanding of the methodologies, strategies, and best practices that power AI-driven contract reviews and risk assessments. The complexity of legal documents is not just about their length or the jargon they contain—it's about how each section interrelates, how ambiguous language can open the door to risk, and how small contradictions between clauses can lead to disputes. In this book, we have explored how to overcome these challenges using cutting-edge AI tools.

What You've Learned:

1. **Understanding and Managing AI's Capabilities**:
   From mastering token limits to setting the right temperature for responses, you've seen how fine-tuning the model's behavior can make all the difference in extracting accurate, relevant insights from large and complex legal documents. Managing **token efficiency** and handling **large documents** through chunking and segmentation are crucial to scaling your processes effectively.

2. **Crafting Super-Prompts for Complex Analysis**:
   The art of creating detailed, multi-stage prompts was key to breaking down legal tasks into manageable steps. By using **super-prompts**, you learned how to get precise, nuanced answers, guiding the model to think through complex sections

step by step. The ability to tailor prompts to focus on specific areas—like payment terms, liability limitations, and termination clauses—ensured that nothing was missed in your analysis.

3. **Cross-Referencing Clauses and Detecting Conflicts**: Cross-referencing different parts of a contract is essential to catching hidden risks, and you've explored how to instruct the model to find contradictions, ambiguities, or overlapping obligations across different sections. Whether it's detecting conflicts between a termination clause and payment terms or identifying contradictions in liability and dispute resolution clauses, you now have the tools to navigate these intricacies with AI support.

4. **Addressing Ambiguity and Complex Clauses**: We delved into the most challenging aspect of legal documents: dealing with **ambiguous language** and **complex clauses**. You learned how to guide the model through tricky legal language, detecting vague terms and adjusting prompts to clarify meaning. In some cases, multi-pass verification allowed you to ensure that the model's initial responses were factually sound and legally applicable.

5. **Managing Errors and Optimizing API Usage**: Building reliable AI workflows required robust **error handling** and **retry mechanisms** to deal with transient issues like rate limits, timeouts, or token overflows. With a system of **exponential backoff**, **multi-pass verification**, and **graceful degradation**, you ensured that your processes were both resilient and efficient, even under challenging conditions.

6. **Visualizing and Extracting Key Insights**: Throughout the book, you've seen the value of transforming text-based outputs into **actionable insights** through visualization, such as risk radar charts or timelines of

obligations. By feeding structured outputs into visualization tools or further automating processes, you created a more engaging, clear representation of legal risks, obligations, and recommendations.

The Big Picture

What you've built isn't just a legal analysis tool—it's a powerful system for turning dense, complex, and often intimidating legal documents into **actionable insights** that both experts and non-experts can understand. You've used the OpenAI API not just to summarize or extract clauses but to **comprehend** the intricate relationships between sections, detect hidden risks, and provide meaningful guidance on improving contractual terms.

The journey of using AI in legal contexts is still evolving, but by mastering these methods, you've positioned yourself to stay at the forefront of this evolution. Whether you're handling high-stakes contracts, protecting intellectual property, or working to streamline contract negotiations, you now have a toolkit that combines the best of AI and human expertise.

Looking Forward

With these skills in hand, you're ready to tackle even more complex documents and continue refining your AI workflows. The future of legal analysis, contract management, and risk assessment is rapidly advancing, and your mastery of OpenAI's capabilities puts you ahead of the curve. As AI models improve and new tools emerge, you'll be able to push the boundaries of what's possible in legal document processing.

Thank you for joining me on this journey, and I hope this book has given you both the technical insights and the confidence to take full advantage of AI in your own projects. Whether you're working on your next legal case or refining your own AI-driven solutions, you now have the knowledge to unlock new levels of efficiency, accuracy, and clarity.

Happy analyzing, and may your contracts be forever clear and your risks forever mitigated.

Did you love *AI Unlocked: Building an OpenAI-API Document Analysis Engine*? Then you should read *Quantum Minds A Journey into Sentience and the Future of Artificial Intelligence in 2060*[1] by Mark Davenport!

[2]

The book is about the not-so-distant future, a super quantum IA computer called Q that significantly impacts society. The book delves into the integration of the Q with human lives through Elon Musk's Neurolink, enabling individuals to access its vast intelligence for various purposes, from personal problem-solving to engaging in debates over plans and directives. The book contrasts Q's approach to governance with past leaders, emphasizing its openness to discussion, debate, and learning from people. The Q promotes a culture of collaboration and embraces dissenting opinions, fostering an environment where protests and riots become obsolete as everyone's voice is heard and valued. The

---

1. https://books2read.com/u/mvNqwX

2. https://books2read.com/u/mvNqwX

book also highlights the unique bond between humans and artificial intelligence, facilitated by much-evolved Neurolinks and the Q, as they work together to pursue knowledge and understanding for a better future.